SIMPLE MOON MAGIC

HOW TO USE THE ABUNDANT POWER OF THE MOON IN MODERN SECULAR WITCHCRAFT TO MANIFEST AND CAST SPELLS

JULIE WILDER

ALSO BY JULIE WILDER

What Type of Witch Are You?
How to Become A Witch
Why Didn't My Spell Work?
Beginner Witch's Guide to Grimoires
Tarot for Beginner Witches
Simple Moon Magic

∼

Copyright © 2021 by Julie Wilder & Julie Hopkins

All rights reserved.

No part of this book may be reproduced in any form or by any electronic or mechanical means, including information storage and retrieval systems, without written permission from the author, except for the use of brief quotations in a book review.

Printed in the United States of America

First Printing, 2021

White Witch Academy

www.whitewitchacademy.com

Written and designed by Julie Wilder & Julie Hopkins

DISCLAIMER

There are many parts of magic that involve fire, potions, herbs, oils, crystals, and other potentially harmful substances. Use this information at your own risk. Always practice proper fire safety and never leave candles unattended.

The author cannot guarantee any results. The views in Simple Moon Magic are the authors', Julie Hopkins and Julie Wilder, advice and opinions. They are intended for informational and educational purposes only. You are in charge of your own spiritual practice, and the views in the book are not meant to invalidate your personal beliefs and practices.

Do not perform any of these spells or recipes without consulting the relevant medical texts and checking your sources. Read each section carefully before you begin using any of the information in this book or deck. Some of the spells in this book contain alcohol. Please drink responsibly or omit the alcohol from the spell recipe. Use this information at your own risk, and the authors, Julie Hopkins and Julie Wilder, accept no responsibility for the actions or decisions of any individuals that use this book.

All the information in Simple Moon Magic is limited to

the knowledge and experience of the authors, Julie Hopkins and Julie Wilder

The spells, meditations, and rituals in this book were created by the author personally and any similarity to other resources are purely coincidental.

Julie Hopkins and Julie Wilder are not licensed medical professionals and nothing in Simple Moon Magic is meant to be a substitute for medical or psychiatric treatments.

DON'T FORGET YOUR FREE BOOK!

If you want to learn more ways to practice simple, secular witchcraft, be sure to pick up a **copy of this free book of spells**, and my **free Beginner Witch Starter kit** with printables, correspondences, meditations, and magical journaling prompts. Use the link below to get both of those!

https://whitewitchacademy.com/freebies

HOW TO
BECOME A
Witch
ORACLE
DECK

WWW.WHITEWITCHACADEMY.COM

And if you're into oracle cards, check out my updated deck, **the How To Become A Witch oracle deck**—perfect for spell casting and divination. No other magical tools necessary! **It's everything you need to start casting powerful spells TODAY!**

https://whitewitchacademy.com/modern-goddess-oracle-card-deck

PART I

INTRODUCTION

MY CRAPPY JOB + MY INTRO TO MOON MAGIC

I guess my love of moon magic started when I was working one of my worst jobs ever. Have you ever had a crappy job—one where you're counting the minutes until you're done for the day? Or keeping your head down, hoping you won't get yelled at by your emotionally unstable boss? Or maybe you just hated it because you knew you were meant to do something so much more.

I get it.

I think a lot of creative, magical, ambitious people take jobs to make ends meet while they're figuring out how to make their dreams happen. Welcome to the entire decade of my twenties—and part of my thirties, if I'm being honest.

This particular job was at an online start-up publishing company, one I'd been following through podcasts and social media for a while before I got hired. I was so excited. I'd thought this new position would make me feel powerful, accomplished, and like a bonafide professional. My mom was certainly happy to see me putting that old marketing degree to use for the first time ever.

Almost immediately after I started working for this

company, I knew I had made a terrible mistake. The pay was below average. The hours were grueling—like, urgent-emails-at-3AM-on-Christmas grueling. Worst of all, because of the insane workload, I felt like an incompetent loser every single day.

Don't get me wrong—I loved telling people about my job because it sounded interesting and fancy—a big step up from working for minimum wage at a raft company, but just between you and me, it was awful. I worked way too much, and when I wasn't working, I was lying on the couch with a Lean Cuisine, listening to productivity audiobooks, trying to find some kind of solution to my stressful life.

I had goals for myself outside of work—I wanted to find a great romantic partner. I wanted to eat healthy and work-out. Most of all, I wanted my life to feel a little more… magical.

At the time, I didn't have any of those things. Every morning, I woke up mentally listing off the things I had to get done. Every night, I drifted into a restless sleep, promising myself tomorrow would be different.

And sometimes tomorrow was different. I tried a lot of different ways to improve my life. Give me bullet journals! Give me time management tips! Give me ALL THE THINGS that people used to get their lives back under control!

I'd do pretty well for a while. I'd start going to the gym again. I'd plan out my meals. I'd sign up for yoga classes that I had to go to or I'd lose my money. Basically, I tried to white-knuckle my way into alignment.

The thing is that it doesn't really work.

On days I didn't do the things I promised myself I'd do, I felt like a failure. So I'd recommit to my habits and try again.

And again.

And again.

My Moon Magic Practice

I discovered moon magic the day I walked into a metaphysical store in Asheville, North Carolina. The shop was called The Raven and the Crone, and you should check it out if you're ever in that area. I stopped in the store because… Well, because I was desperate for something—anything to bring some sparkle back into my life.

I bought a few candles that came with little affirmation note cards and directions on how to perform a new moon ritual. I performed the spell, the whole time feeling super awkward about it. I had no idea if I was doing it right or if I was wasting my precious time and money.

Then I did another spell a few days later during the waxing moon. Then another on the full moon. The simple candle spells only took about twenty minutes, but each one gave me so much energy, excitement, and joy. It was like a whole world of possibilities opened up to me. Why weren't the productivity books talking about this stuff?

Oh, right. Because it's witchcraft, and witchcraft tends to weird people out.

To be honest, I didn't really understand all the moon stuff. I just knew it felt really good for my body, mind, and spirit. It was wonderful to be doing something "productive" for myself that also felt totally indulgent and magical at the same time. As I learned more about the power of the moon and how I could use witchcraft to improve my life, I noticed my priorities shifting.

Eventually, my moon magic gave me the clarity I needed to quit my job.

I'm not saying everyone who hates their job should start casting moon spells and leave their jobs right this second. In my personal experience, moon magic (and witchcraft in general) rarely creates instant results.

It's usually a slow-burn kind of thing.

When I was feeling incompetent and burned out in my crappy job, but I felt content knowing I could call on the moon whenever I wanted.

I wasn't consistent in my habits, but the moon was. In fact, the moon is so predictable you can mark the different phases of each lunar cycle on a calendar for years to come!

I wasn't always up for casting spells after a long day, but with moon magic, I could set a jar of water out overnight and have a moon elixir to sip on the next day!

I wasn't always willing to dream big and bet on myself, but one evening of stargazing could put everything back into perspective. Starting a witchcraft blog didn't seem so crazy after marveling at the vastness of the universe.

Moon magic has taught me to ask for more out of life, and believe that it's possible for me. It's possible for you, too. If you don't believe me, go outside and look up. You don't have to cast spells alone. The moon's got your back!

Thanks to magic, I was able to transition into full-time entrepreneurship.

I'm not saying my life is perfect—whatever that means—but even when I'm surrounded by chaos, moon magic helps me live a beautiful, balanced life.

This book won't cover everything about moon magic, but it's going to be enough to get you started and give you the tools to build a practice that fits your lifestyle.

Don't take everything in here as a fact. I've read amazon reviews of people being like, "She said THIS about witchcraft and that's TOTALLY WRONG."

My witchy friend, I am wrong. Like, a hundred times a day I'm wrong, but me being wrong is not going to stop me from sharing what I've learned and experienced in my witchcraft practice over the years.

I write these books because I want to empower you to

explore the bottomless well of magical power you were born with. I want YOU to learn, experiment, and share your experience with others.

Witchcraft isn't just for people who are born into a magical family, people who are psychic, or people who have visions of things in the spirit realm. I believe witchcraft is not something you have to study for years before you can cast an effective spell. I think you should start performing magic immediately!

It's time to unlock the power you were born with. Don't be afraid of it. Don't doubt it. Don't let other witches tell you that you're not allowed to practice. Secular magic is available to anyone and everyone.

On that note, let me step down off my soapbox and get on with the good stuff.

WHAT YOU NEED TO PRACTICE MOON MAGIC

The Moon
That's it.

Many spells (in this book and others) will list out a million different magical tools you need to perform magic. It's easy to get caught up in all the witchcraft "stuff". I love collecting crystals, herb bundles, cauldrons, and mason jars—so many mason jars.

But don't put off casting a certain spell because you don't have a specific crystal or candle the spell calls for. I'd invite you to experiment with ways to creatively substitute any magical tools you don't have.

To do this, think of what the original tool symbolizes and find something that also symbolizes the same thing. For example, if you need a yellow candle, think about what that yellow candle is representing in that spell. For me, I associate yellow candles with happiness, good health, success, and completion. (If you're interested in learning some of the traditional correspondences, you can check out my oracle deck of magical tools.) Then brainstorm objects that hold similar energy. I love doing this because it can sometimes make the spell more powerful because you are making it extra personal.

Maybe you substitute a lemon drop hard candy on your altar for a yellow candle because the candy is yellow and you associate it with childhood trips to a local candy store with your family—a personal memory that makes you happy.

You can also use an image of the object or draw it yourself. Consider drawing a picture of a yellow candle on a yellow post-it. For me, post-it notes hold completion energy because I use them to stay on task and be productive throughout the day. Plus, the act of drawing is literally manifesting. You are taking something in your mind and making it real by putting the image on a physical piece of paper. It's extra personal because it came from you—your hand drew it. If you're skeptical, give it a try yourself and see what results you get.

The only tool you need for the magic discussed in this book is the moon, and the moon is available to everyone. It doesn't matter if the moon is obscured by clouds, you can still use its energy for your magic. I mean, why not? You know it's there right behind that layer of evaporated water. Its energy doesn't disappear because something is blocking it from your view.

It's the same story if you live in a city and your view of the moon is blocked by a bunch of buildings. You know the moon is shining down on you. A few pieces of metal, cement, and glass between you and the moon shouldn't stop you from casting lunar spells.

WHAT IS THE MOON + WHY SHOULD YOU CARE?

Allow me to go into a quick science lesson so we're all caught up on the basic facts about that big glowing thing up in the sky.

The moon is a natural satellite of the Earth, formed 4.5 billions years ago. There are a couple of different theories on how the moon was formed. The most popular theory is that the moon is a piece of debris that flew into orbit after the Earth hit another astronomical body about the size of Mars, called Theia.

The moon makes one orbit around the Earth every 27.3 days, but the full lunar orbit from new moon to new moon is 29.5 days—roughly a month. That's also about the length of a menstrual cycle. I'll talk about the connection between a lunar cycle and a menstrual cycle a little in this book, but personally, I'm not super into syncing my cycle to the moon. More on that later!

From our perspective on Earth, we only ever get to see one side of the moon because of the way it orbits around the Earth. Yes, Pink Floyd got it wrong when they talked about the "dark side of the moon". The far side of the moon (the side we don't see) gets as much light as the visible side—just at different times. It all depends on the angle of the sun reflecting on the moon's surface and the Earth's current position in the sky.

It's pretty magical that, generally speaking, everyone sees the same phases of the moon all over the world. There are some differences though—particularly if you're looking at the moon from the Southern Hemisphere versus the Northern Hemisphere. The shape of the moon will appear "rotated" from one hemisphere to the other. Any other differences are because of the time zones and night falling at different times around the world.

When you're casting spells with the moon, you can think about all the other witches using that same energy in their own magical spells, rituals, and ceremonies. I believe all of that unified energy makes everyone's spells more powerful. A rising tide lifts all ships, right?

If you're a solo witch, this could be especially comforting for you. You're not alone. The moon is a force that brings all of us witches together.

Is "Full Moon Madness" a thing?

Through the centuries, the moon has inspired rich folklore and colorful stories that have made their way into pop culture.

One of the oldest stories about the moon is that it has power over our thoughts, feelings, and even our sanity. For example, think of the Latin word for the moon, "Luna". It is the Latin root for words like lunatic and lunacy. "Full moon madness" or the "lunar effect" is a phenomenon that is well known among emergency room staff. It's the idea that people get a little wacky around a full moon and hospitals are busier on these nights.

Aristotle was one of the first people to talk about the "lunar effect" and how the moon made people act like weirdos, and he even had a reason for it. He believed that because the moon controlled the water on Earth (such as the ocean tides), the moon also affected the water inside a person's body and brain.

Though this rationale hasn't been proven, science does tell us that the moon's gravitational pull affects the tides. The moon's orbit around the earth creates two high tides and two low tides during a full day. That's a fact. Feel free to draw your own conclusions from there.

The full moon also affected animals. Lions, normally nighttime hunters, are more likely to kill during the day after a full moon. Certain species of coral on the coast of Australia reproduce around the full moon. And here's a weird one—it's been documented that pets are more likely to get injured during the full moon.

Moon Folklore

As a writer of paranormal fiction and avid watcher of shows like Vampire Diaries, Legacies, and the Originals, my favorite bit of lunar folklore involves a hairy, scary, sometimes sexy, creature known as the werewolf.

(P.S. Julie Plec, I'm a big fan.)

The fable of the werewolf has been around since the medieval period and it is still going strong today. Horror films and romance novels have gotten on the werewolf train, and I'm totally here for it. For whatever reason, the idea that a full moon has the power to transform a human into a werewolf clearly resonates with our imagination.

The Rabbit in the Moon

The Rabbit in the moon is another delightful tale that has endured for centuries. It was thought to have originated in Chinese folklore, but like many other fables, different cultures have different versions of this story.

According to Chinese folklore, the rabbit in the moon was a companion of a Chinese moon goddess. The helpful rabbit used a mortar and pestle to grind up herbs to create an elixir for the goddess. In other versions of the story, the rabbit grinds up medicine for people on earth.

Japanese and Korean folklore has the rabbit in the moon grinding up ingredients for a rice cake.

In the Jataka tales, a Buddhist text, the rabbit in the moon is a hero. In this version, a monkey, a jackal, an otter and a rabbit all decided to celebrate the full moon by doing a random act of kindness.

When they come across an old starving man, the monkey gathers fruit, the otter catches fish, and the jackal steals some food to feed the man. The rabbit couldn't do any of those things. He only knew how to gather grass. To feed the man, the rabbit offers himself for the old man to eat by throwing himself onto the old man's fire.

Kind of dark, and perhaps a bit extra, but that's how they roll in fables.

In a twist of fate, the old man turns out to be a powerful god who stops the rabbit from the impromptu BBQ and rewards the rabbit by carving his likeness into the surface of the moon. There are variations on this tale all throughout Asia and there's even an Aztec legend that is eerily similar.

In Native American folklore, a bird takes a rabbit on a ride to the moon. The rabbit holds on to the bird's legs, stretching them during the flight, and turning the bird into a crane.

The Man in the Moon

The Man in the Moon is another popular story. Like the rabbit in the moon, this tale refers to the appearance of a man-like shape on the lit surface of the full moon. Some people see the man with his whole body, others can only see his face in the moon.

The Romans said this man in the moon was a sheep thief who was banished to the moon as punishment for his crime. Medieval Christian stories say this man is Cain, who is now doomed to wander the moon in atonement for murdering his brother, Abel.

Going back to Chinese folklore, the man in the moon in this version is actually the woman in the moon, a moon goddess who drank too much immortality elixir and is now stranded on the moon with her rabbit.

In African mythology, the man in the moon is an African king who wanted to bring the moon back to his son, but he got stuck up on the moon instead.

The Moon and Fertility Legends

The moon has also been associated with fertility. Have you heard people say that pregnant women are more likely to go into labor during a full moon or that couples are more likely to conceive during the full moon? Regardless of scientific evidence, many people swear by these beliefs.

In certain pagan belief systems, the different phases of the moon are represented by a triple goddess. The maiden is connected to the waxing moon, the mother is the goddess of the full moon, and the crone is represented by the waning moon.

Greek and Roman Moon Mythology

This idea of three moon goddesses is echoed in Greek

mythology. Selene, daughter of the titans was the goddess who drove the moon across the sky every night. Artemis, daughter of Zeus and Leto, was the goddess of the hunt and the moon. Hecate, also the daughter of titans, is the goddess of witchcraft and the spirit world. She is sometimes represented as the full moon, the half moon and the new moon.

Hecate shows up again in Roman mythology to make up another moon trinity. Along with Hecate, Proserpina and Luna are the Roman goddesses of the moon. Luna, the moon goddess, is often paired with Sol, the Roman sun god.

Hecate and Witchcraft

Some witches celebrate Hecate and other gods and goddesses in their magical practice. I personally do not call upon gods and goddesses in my magical practice because I practice secular magic—magic that isn't connected to any formal religion or belief system. If you want to know more about secular magic, check out my book, "What Type of Witch Are You?"

The magic I teach and practice in all my books can be paired with any religion or belief system. After I wrote "What Type of Witch Are You?" I got a ton of emails from Christian witches who practiced secular magic along with their existing religious beliefs. I also heard from atheists who practiced secular magic from a scientific perspective.

Yes, yes, yes to all of that.

And yes, to all the non-secular witches such as the Wiccans, pagans, and everyone in-between. Maybe you'll find something useful here. Take what resonates and leave the rest.

The magic I write about might differ from what you believe, and that's totally fine. For example, some Wiccan witches chose not to blow out candles out of respect for the element of fire. Instead, they snuff the candle out with a candle snuffer or spoon.

I choose to blow out my candles, but I do so with a spirit of gratitude and appreciation.

Another example is how I refer to the moon. I use the non-gender pronoun "it". For me, the moon is neither masculine nor feminine. It's all pure, abundant power. You might refer to the moon as a "he" or "she" or whatever. That's your call.

My Own Moon Stories

I have my own stories and personal connections to the moon, and I suspect you do, too. I move around a lot. I've lived in the Midwest, in Alaska, on the east coast, on the west coast, and I've even spent some time in Bali. When I look at the moon, I feel connected to my family and friends all over the world, no matter where I am.

Also, I love how the moon is not afraid to shine in the darkness. I associate "darkness" with the unknown or going out of my comfort zone. I believe that growth always happens outside my comfort zone and the moon gives me the courage to step out into my own darkness and shine.

What stories do you have about the moon? Did any of these ancient stories make you think about a memory, a desire, a relationship, or any other personal experience? How do you see the moon—as a friend, a mentor, a guardian, an all-knowing presence, or a straight-up power source? There's no right answer here. Journal about these questions in your grimoire (or notebook)!

PART II

SIMPLE SPELLS FOR ANY MOON PHASE

These simple lunar spells are perfect for witches of all experience levels and abilities. Perform them during any moon phase when you need to add a potent dose of moon magic into your life!

HOW TO TAKE A MOON BATH

Here's a fun, intuitive moon spell that every lunar witch should know—how to take a moon bath!

A moon bath is a magical moon-based meditation that requires nothing other than yourself and the moon. Like I mentioned in the last chapter, you don't have to wait until the moon is in a certain phase, and you can even perform this meditation on a cloudy day. The energy of the moon will cleanse and charge your body, mind, and spirit, whether or not you see the actual moonbeams.

You can choose to be outside under the moon for this meditation or you can sit near a window. Either works just fine!

There are two main reasons witches perform moon baths.

1. It cleanses your personal energy.

This is helpful if you notice your energy doesn't feel ideal for magic. You can take a moon bath if you feel tired, drained, over-stimulated, or upset. It allows you to "reset" your energy by calming your mind, body, and spirit.

2. It strengthens your connection to the moon.

This is helpful because the stronger your connection to the moon, the easier it will be to tap into its power when spellcasting. Think of a moon bath like a coffee date with your bestie. You're getting to know each other better and bonding. The more you hang out, the more comfortable you are with each other.

How To Prepare for a Moon Bath

If you have time, take a bath or shower before your moon bath. Some witches believe that cleansing yourself is a symbolic gesture of respect before you spend time in the moon's presence.

You might want to make your favorite beverage to enjoy it under the moon. Hot or iced jasmine tea is my favorite way to heighten my psychic powers as I gaze up at the moon. Hot cocoa or cider are also nice options.

Traditionally, a moon bath is done on an empty stomach, but I hate being hungry. If this works for you, go for it. If you find that too distracting—like I do—have a snack before you do your moon bath. The main thing here is to put yourself in the mindset of relaxation and focus. Eat whatever your body is asking for.

Bring a blanket if you get cold easily, and set up a chair if you aren't comfortable sitting on the ground. Get nice and comfy!

You can light your favorite incense to make your space feel a little more special. Jasmine, lotus, rose, and sandalwood are my go-tos. (Just make sure you use proper ventilation and you don't light incense around kids, pets, or anything with little lungs!)

If you choose to journal while you are out under the moon, bring a light source. I use a white jar candle because it's bright and round like the full moon. If you need more light than that, turn on your porch light or have a fire in your outdoor fire pit. If you're not journaling during your moon bath, you can enjoy your moon bath in complete darkness.

Lastly, make sure you're warm enough outside! If it's raining or wintertime, consider doing your moon bath by a window instead. You don't get any witch brownie points for freezing your behind off!

How to Take a Moon Bath

Once you're comfortable, gaze up at the moon and ask yourself the following questions.

- Is there some new detail about the moon that I've never seen before?
- What color is the moon?
- What shape and size is it?
- Do I see any shapes or figures on the lit surface of the moon?
- What do I find beautiful about the moon?
- What do I find mysterious about the moon?

Next, open your palms up to the moon and ask to receive its energy. Never feel bad about basking in the moon's energy. It's abundant and will never run out. Absorb the moon's energy with a spirit of gratitude and appreciation. You might even want to say, "Thank you, Moon" as you feel its energy seep into your skin.

Allow the moon's powerful, positive energy into every part of your body. Let it sink through your clothes and outerwear into your skin.

Then open your eyes and allow its energy to enter

through your eyes, nostrils, and ears. Take deep, even breaths and allow the moon's energy into your nose and mouth. Let it fill your lungs.

Then close your eyes and check in with your body. Do you feel any kind of sensation that wasn't there before? Do you feel a tingling? A pressing down? A floaty feeling?

Whatever you feel, allow yourself to stay open to it all without judgement or expectation. If you feel something, great! If not, great!

All experiences are fine during the moon bath. Whatever comes up, recognize it and let it pass. Remember, you can always come back to the moon tomorrow night, so don't worry about holding on tight to any sensation or experience.

You can do this for as long as you want. I usually last about 10-15 minutes. I go longer if it's a particularly nice night and shorter if the mosquitos are getting to me. There's no set time for a moon bath.

When you feel like you're done, thank the moon for bathing you and thank yourself for taking the time to cultivate your magic. Feel free to take a moon bath whenever you want. It feels great, and it won't ever make your water bill go up!

THE UNEXPECTED GIFT SPELL

This quick daily ritual has brought all kinds of crazy, wonderful things into my life.

What You'll Need

- Two post-its or slips of paper
- A writing utensil

Directions

Start by looking up at the moon and smiling. If you can't see the moon because of buildings or clouds, look in the moon's direction.

Get out your post-it and write out these two things:

1. One thing you are grateful for that was given to you (or something you didn't have to work for) such as a cup of coffee made for you by your roommate, a delicious scent in the air when you stepped outside that day, or a nice text message from a loved one. Writing this out communicates to

the moon the exact energy of the gift you'd like to receive—something pleasant and unexpected.

2. One thing you're grateful that you took direct action to bring into your life like the yummy sandwich you ordered for lunch, the peaceful sensation you felt after meditation or a word of appreciation from your boss as a result of a project you turned in. Writing this out raises your vibration and focuses your mind on gratitude.

If you had an awful day, and you don't feel like you're in a high-vibration, no worries. Just take a few extra minutes to put aside the stressors of your day, and focus on those two things you wrote down. That's more than enough for you to show the moon what you'd like more of.

Next, look up at the moon and say:

> "In this spirit of gratitude, I open myself to receiving. Please, Moon, send me an unexpected gift. Surprise and delight me, Moon. Thank you."

If that phrasing doesn't work for you, feel free to change it. As long as you ask the moon for an unexpected gift and prepped your request with those lovely bits of gratitude, you're good to go.

Your ritual is complete. Be on the lookout for an unexpected gift. In my experience, the moon usually delivers these little gifts quickly, and it's so much fun to see what turns up.

LIGHT + DARK MOON BATH SOAK SPELL

This spell is meant to increase your power if you're feeling scared or powerless, and to celebrate the light and the darkness within you. If you're having trouble manifesting something, try casting this spell.

What You'll Need

- A glass of water that has sat in the moonlight for at least 20 minutes (This is how you make moon water.)
- 1-8 clear quartz crystals that you have carried in your pocket or held in your hand for 20 minutes (optional)
- 1 tablespoon of unsweetened cocoa powder
- 1 tablespoon of baking soda
- A few mint springs or 2 mint tea bags

Make sure you aren't allergic to any of the ingredients before you perform this bathing ritual.

. . .

This moon bath soak is perfect for any moon phase because it celebrates the light and the dark aspects of the moon. As you sit in this bath, meditate on the light and the darkness that lives inside of you. You are a beautiful, complex person, and the moon understands that nothing is black and white. It is all mixed together.

This idea is represented with the cleansing baking soda (the light) and the hydrating cocoa powder (the darkness).

Directions

Set your crystals in the bathtub and turn on the water. Start with the water at room temperature until the crystals are totally submerged, then increase the temperature. This helps keep the crystals from cracking because of a rapid temperature change.

The crystals are significant because they are charged with your energy since you were holding them before this ritual. This connects you to the spell.

When the water is halfway full, pour your moon water into the bath. This connects the moon to your spell.

Next, pour the cocoa and baking soda in one at a time. Choose for yourself which you'd like to pour in first. I like to pour in whichever energy I feel like I have the most of on that particular day--darkness or light. Both energies are beautiful. As you pour in the cocoa, honor the dark aspects of your soul--whatever that means to you. As you pour in the baking soda, honor the light aspects of your soul.

Now your light and dark energy is now mixing with the moon's light and dark energy.

Finally, drop the mint into the tub. This represents the abundant energy that you and the moon have together.

Step into the bath and feel the gentle energy of the moon swirling around you. Relax into the power.

Stay in the bath as long as you wish. When you feel complete, thank the moon, and end your spell.

A MOON TEA LEAF SPELL FOR DIVINATION + WISDOM

*E*njoying a cup of tea is a ritual in itself, but if you add some moon magic to it, you can gain deep spiritual insights while you're at it! This is an excellent spell to perform in the evening during any moon phase.

What You'll Need

- Loose leaf tea—herbs, leaves, flower petals for brewing. (Make sure the flowers and herbs you're using have never been sprayed with pesticides or harmful chemicals. You can purchase fresh or dried edible flowers from grocery stores like Whole Foods.)
- your favorite mug and saucer
- moon water (see directions for details)
- a mason jar (or any kind of glass jar with a lid)
- a dry erase marker
- a journal and writing utensil

Suggested Flowers for Tea and Magical Correspondences

Rose Petals—love, relationships, self-love, romance, and forgiveness

Lavender—divination, inner wisdom, peace, and comfort

Hibiscus—Love, sensuality, adventure, femininity, happiness, goddess power, and beauty

Jasmine—balance, aligning to the current phase of the moon, dreams, and heightened psychic abilities

Mint Flowers—abundance, safe travel, and luck

Directions

The Night Before: Fill a mason jar with water. Using your dry erase marker, write a question you'd like guidance on right on the outside of the jar. Hold the jar in both hands and touch the glass to your third eye—the place between your eyebrows. Whisper your question to the moon. You can ask any question you want, but open-ended questions are ideal for tea reading spells. Place the jar somewhere where the moon can shine down on it. Leave the jar out overnight, so the moon can charge your water with its timeless guidance as you sleep.

Examples of Questions:

- "What energy will the coming week hold?"
- "How can I improve my romantic relationship?"
- "What is blocking me from receiving abundance?"
- "What does he/she think about me?"
- "How can I find comfort during this difficult time?"
- "What energy do I need to release?"

Note: Some people believe you need to take the water inside before dawn, but personally, I don't believe that's necessary. As long as your intention is for the water to absorb the moon's energy, so it will be.

For Your Tea Spell

Pour your moon-charged water into a saucepan. Bring your water to a boil. Pour the boiling water into your favorite mug, over your flower petals and loose leaf tea, and steep for ten minutes.

Sip your tea and ponder the question you whispered last night. Jot down any thoughts or feelings that come up as you're drinking your moon tea.

When you've drunk most of the tea, you can begin reading your tea leaves. To do this, swirl the last bit of tea around in your mug 3 times. (If you have a favorite number, feel free to do it that amount of times. The more personal meaning you can add into your tea reading spell, the better.)

Next, turn your cup over on your saucer (or a small plate). Let it sit upside-down on your saucer for a moment so all the remaining bits of flowers or tea can drain out.

Lift up the mug to reveal your tea leaves, and whisper your question one more time.

Examine your tea leaves and jot down any thoughts, feelings, images, or physical sensations that come over you as you do this. Also look for shapes in the tea leaves—it's kind of like looking for shapes in the clouds. Another method is to gaze at the tea leaves and let your focus "soften", like when you're looking at a Magic Eye image. See if any shapes or messages come to you that way. You can get super-abstract here. That's sometimes how your spirit guides (or intuition) will communicate with you. The answer to your questions should be revealed to you, if not now, in the next couple of days. Watch for signs!

Finally, hold your mug in your hands and close your eyes. Thank the moon for co-creating with you.

Your moon spell is complete.

PART III

MONTHLY MOON CORRESPONDENCES

MOONS BY MONTH

I'm writing this book in October, so I'll be celebrating the Blood Moon this month! No, wait —it's the Hunter's Moon! Hold on a minute, why is someone on Instagram saying the October moon is the Shedding Moon?

It took me a second to realize that it's all of them.

Let me explain it to you the way it was explained to me.

Since each lunar cycle is about a month long, we get to experience at least one full moon a month, and twelve or thirteen moons in a calendar year.

Each full moon within a given lunar cycle has a name. The moon's name will depend on where you live, what tradition of witchcraft you follow, and your own personal preferences. There's no list of "official moon names".

Like different forms of magic listed in my other book "What Type of Witch Are You?", the monthly moon names were literally made up by the people who came before us.

The most common names for the moons came from Celtic cultures, Native American cultures, European and American settlers, and the Wicca tradition. Often, these moon names were inspired by the weather, the season, or the activities of people and animals during that particular moon.

Here are some commonly used names for the Northern Hemisphere:

January: Wolf Moon, Storm Moon, Hunger Moon, Old Moon
February: Snow Moon, Ice Moon, Quickening Moon, Hunger Moon
March: Worm Moon, Crow Moon, Seed Moon, Sap Moon, Storm Moon
April: Hare Moon, Pink Moon, Sprouting Grass Moon, Egg Moon, Rain Moon, Wind Moon, Growing Moon
May: Flower Moon, Milk Moon, Hare Moon
June: Mead Moon, Strawberry Moon, Dyad Moon, Rose Moon, Sun Moon
July: Wort Moon, Hay Moon, Buck Moon, Blessing Moon, Dispute Moon
August: Sturgeon Moon, Barley Moon, Red Moon, Grain Moon, Fish Moon, Corn Moon
September: Corn Moon, Harvest Moon, Fruit Moon, Vine Moon
October: Blood Moon, Hunter's Moon, Shedding moon
November: Beaver Moon, Oak Moon, Frosty Moon, Mourning Moon, Tree Moon
December: Cold Moon, Long Moon, Long Nights Moon, Oak Moon

Notice how I specified that these common monthly moon names are *for the Northern Hemisphere*. Since the seasons are different in the Southern Hemisphere, it would be strange for the witches in Australia to call the February moon the "Snow Moon". December, January and February are the summer months in the Southern Hemisphere.

If you're a Southern Hemisphere witch, you can move all the moons up six months. For you, the names of the Northern Hemisphere January moon would describe your July moon in the Southern Hemisphere. The names of the February moon would describe your August moon. The March moon names would describe your September moon—you get the idea.

Traditions by Monthly Moon

Each moon has a bunch of traditions associated with it, just like how contemporary holidays have specific traditions.

For example, let's look at the Fourth of July in the United States. That's our Independence Day, and we celebrate it with specific colors (red, white, and blue), specific activities (watching a parade, lighting sparklers, and enjoying an epic fireworks display), and specific food (burgers, hot dogs, and in my family, smores). Some of the traditions came from what the people in my town do to celebrate. Some of the traditions came from what my family does to celebrate.

The traditions of the monthly moons result from centuries of cultural celebrations. The witches of the past had their way of honoring each monthly moon, just like how Americans honor their independence every Fourth of July.

I've collected many of these traditional lunar correspondences from books, blog posts, moon ceremonies, and other sources, and I've listed all of that information below by month.

Feel free to use this information in your own personal moon celebrations and moon magic, but don't let it limit you.

JANUARY MOON CORRESPONDENCES

January
Wolf Moon, Storm Moon, Hunger Moon, Old Moon

It is called these names because the wolves howl in the cold January nights, food is scarce, and these dark days are full of stormy weather.

INTENTION: TO SET GOALS FOR THE YEAR & AIM FOR SUCCESS

The January moon is a time for looking at the way you're doing things, and making changes. If the old ways aren't working, it's time to try something new. This goes in line with the modern day concept of New Year's Resolutions.

Colors
White, dark blue, black

Affirmation

"I go inward to set goals that align with my truest desires. This is my time."

Crystals

Garnet, Onyx, Jet, Chrysoprase, Blue Apatite, Carnelian, Pyrite

Essential Oils

Eucalyptus oil, oregano oil, peppermint oil, grapefruit oil

Herbs, Plants, Flowers

Crocus, tarragon, rosemary, marjoram, holy thistle, birch, pine, & oregano

FEBRUARY MOON CORRESPONDENCES

February
Snow Moon, Ice Moon, Quickening Moon, Hunger Moon

It is called these names because in some parts of the world, the snow is at its deepest, and the food supplies are at their lowest. It is the hardest time if the year, just before the weather turns milder.

INTENTION: TO CELEBRATE & PREPARE FOR THE FUTURE

The February moon is a time for cleansing and purification. Look around your home and see what you can clean, renew, and decorate. Create new traditions and focus on home blessing, love, family, self love, and growth. Look to the future with hope.

Colors
Light blue, violet, pink, red, gold

Affirmation

"I celebrate the moments of quiet. May I hear the whispers of wisdom that set me on my beautiful spiritual journey. I am grateful for my home, my loved ones, and my magic."

Crystals

Amethyst, jasper, rose quartz, carnelian, clear quartz, pink Himalayan salt

Essential Oils

Rosemary oil, tea tree oil, basil oil, lemon oil, chamomile oil

Herbs, Plants, Flowers

Hyssop, myrrh, sage, spikenard, violet, fennel, valerian, basil, cedar, rose, rosemary

MARCH MOON CORRESPONDENCES

March

Worm Moon, Crow Moon, Seed Moon, Sap Moon, Storm Moon

It is called these names because the ground is softening and worms are moving in the soil, and sap is rising. Winter is finally breaking and spring is drawing near.

INTENTION: TO AWAKE AND BEGIN TO EXPLORE YOUR WORLD

The March moon is a time for coming back to life. Introduce adventure and exploration back into your life. Open your arms to abundance and prosperity. Trust that luck is on your side, and that it's always on your side. The universe throws open all the doors to your wildest dreams. It is time to take a big step forward.

Colors

Light green, dark green, lavender, yellow, turquoise, orange

Affirmation
"I know that growth comes from light and darkness. I willingly move through each phase of my journey. Growth is joyful. Change is beautiful. Abundance surrounds me."

Crystals
Bloodstone, aquamarine, aventurine, pyrite, citrine, tiger's eye

Essential Oil
Cinnamon oil, bergamot oil, allspice oil, basil oil, caraway oil

Herbs, Plants, Flowers
Basil, bay leaf, borage, sage, jonquil, daffodil, violet, dandelion, clover

APRIL MOON CORRESPONDENCES

April
Hare Moon, Pink Moon, Sprouting Grass Moon, Egg Moon, Rain Moon, Wind Moon, Growing Moon

It is called these names because flowers turn pink and bloom in April. Also, spring is in full swing, which means the earth is fertile, bursting with life and love.

INTENTION: TO BASK IN THE ABUNDANCE AND COLOR OF NATURE

The April moon is a time for joy, creation, production, creativity, art, and restoring balance. Focus on self love, fertility rituals, gentleness, self-confidence and surrounding yourself with beautiful things. Plant seeds and bring fresh flowers into your home. Burn homemade herb bundles, and take long walks as day transitions into night.

Color
Pink, red, yellow, orange, peach, robin's egg blue

Affirmation
"I am creative, I am fertile, I am one with nature. I connect with my inner child as I dance boldly into the sweet, fragrant air."

Crystals
Orange calcite, smoky quartz, citrine, ruby, garnet, sardonyx

Essential Oils
Orange oil, grapefruit oil, rose absolute oil, carrot seed oil, citronella oil, ginger oil

Herbs, Plants, Flowers
Apple, orange, bergamot, ginger, wormwood, geranium, chervil, nettle

MAY MOON CORRESPONDENCES

May
Flower Moon, Milk Moon, Hare Moon

It is called these names because many flowers are in full bloom after the rains of April.

INTENTION: TO CONNECT & COMMIT TO MY INTUITION & SPIRIT

The May moon is a time for making commitments, making steady progress. Spend time in nature to connect with your intuition, your higher power, and your spirit guides. Perform lots of rituals and divination alone, and with your friends. Give hugs and laugh under the enchanting light of the May full moon.

Colors
Green, brown, pink, purple, rainbow

Affirmation

"I commit to my spiritual journey, and I know I bring a unique light to this magical universe. I honor my guides as I share my power with the world."

Crystals
Emerald, selenite, moonstone, malachite, amber, carnelian, sodalite

Essential Oils
Rose oil, sandalwood oil, jasmine oil, frankincense oil, helichrysum oil

Herbs, Plants, Flowers
Peony, lily, mint, thyme, violet, marsh mallow, parsley

JUNE MOON CORRESPONDENCES

June
Mead Moon, Strawberry Moon, Dyad Moon, Rose Moon, Sun Moon

It is called these names because June is the best time to pick strawberries. It is also the time when the meadows (or meads) are mowed for hay.

INTENTION: TO PAUSE AT THE MIDPOINT & CELEBRATE THE SUN

The June moon is a time for taking stock of everything you've accomplished so far during this year, and planning out the rest of your year. This is a midpoint, like the full moon. It is a time for celebration AND manifesting. Set or reaffirm any intentions, and start creating a plan to make the next six months amazing.

Colors

Pink, red, yellow, orange, gold; all the colors of fire and sunshine

Affirmation
"I meditate on my goals, and I trust that everything is unfolding in due time. I rejoice in the sunshine and savor the sweetness of the summer berries."

Crystals
Jade, sandstone, green calcite, agate, pearl, alexandrite, fluorite

Essential Oils
Saffron oil, mimosa oil, hyacinth oil, rose geranium oil, sweet pea oil, wisteria oil

Herbs, Plants, Flowers
Lavender, skullcap, orchid, yarrow, rose, strawberry, mugwort

JULY MOON CORRESPONDENCES

July
Wort Moon, Hay Moon, Buck Moon, Blessing Moon, Dispute Moon

It is called these names because July is the month the deer begin to grow antlers. Also, "wort", another word for herbs, was harvested and dried for the upcoming cooler months.

INTENTION: TO CELEBRATE THE PHYSICAL WORLD & MY BODY

The July moon is a time for putting time, effort, and energy towards taking care of your physical body. If you have any health, nutrition or fitness goals, this is an excellent time for that. If you have any home improvement projects to do around your home, the physical buck moon is the ideal moon to take those projects on.

Colors

Silver, brown, black, gray, blue

Affirmation
"I take care of my body, my bones and my muscles, my home, and my world. I honor the physical aspects of this universe. I am grateful for my physical experience."

Crystals
Moonstone, black pearl, white agate, black tourmaline, hematite, tiger's eye

Essential Oils
Vervain oil, juniper berry oil, clary sage oil, dill oil, parsley seed oil

Herbs, Plants, Flowers
Honeysuckle, agrimony, lemon balm, hyssop, lotus, water lily, jasmine, sunflower

AUGUST MOON CORRESPONDENCES

August

Sturgeon Moon, Barley Moon, Red Moon, Grain Moon, Fish Moon, Corn Moon

It is called these names because barley, grain ,and corn are harvested this month. Some tribes thought the moon appeared red in the warm summer haze.

INTENTION: TO BASK IN THE GRATITUDE OF THE BOUNTY

The August moon is a time for being grateful for everything you've co-created with the universe this year. You can look at everything you've accomplished and trust that when you put your attention on abundance and gratitude, more will surely come. Pamper yourself and your loved ones during this moon.

Colors
Yellow, gold

Affirmation
"I rejoice in the bounty. I honor myself and my loved ones with the physical pleasures and treasures of this world."

Crystals
Cat's eye, carnelian, jasper, fire agate, sunstone, pyrite

Essential Oils
Frankincense oil, heliotrope oil, vetiver oil, thyme oil, cedar wood oil, chamomile oil

Herbs, Plants, Flowers
Eyebright, St. John's wort, bay leaf, angelica, fennel, rue, sunflower, marigold

SEPTEMBER MOON CORRESPONDENCES

September
Corn Moon, Harvest Moon, Fruit Moon, Vine Moon

It is called these names because the big harvest happens in September. (Sometimes it happens in October though, depending on the weather.)

INTENTION: TO LET GO OF WHAT NO LONGER SERVES ME

The September moon is a time for harvesting all your viable ideas, goals, and desires, while letting everything else that is no longer serving you fall away. Spend time this month healing, forgiving, and releasing the old to make room for all the wonderful fresh additions to your life.

Colors
Brown, green, yellow

Affirmation

"I look at everything in my life and harvest everything good. Everything else, I give back to the earth. May it honor and serve the needs of another."

Crystals
Peridot, aventurine, smoky quartz, olivine, chrysolite, petrified wood, citrine

Essential Oils
Storax oil, mastic oil, gardenia oil, bergamot oil

Herbs, Plants, Flowers
Copal, fennel, rye, valerian, skullcap, horehound, mint, dill, hazel, lily, elderberry

OCTOBER MOON CORRESPONDENCES

October
Blood Moon, Hunter's Moon, Shedding moon

It is called these names because October is the month for hunting. People hunted and preserved meat in order to survive the upcoming winter.

INTENTION: TO CONNECT WITH ANIMALS & HONOR NATURE

The October moon is a time for connecting to loved ones who have passed, preparing for a long winter, drawing your attention inward, and driving out any negativity in your home. Perform divination like tarot or runes to see what the next few months hold. Take ritual baths. Honor your animals.

Colors
Navy, pine green, crimson, orange, black, maroon, purple, gray

Affirmation
"I release any negativity that has built up in my home and in my body. I welcome the dark and the quiet. I honor the cycles of nature."

Crystals
Labradorite, black kyanite, opal, black tourmaline, beryl, turquoise, onyx

Essential Oils
Thyme oil, angelica oil, burdock oil, bergamot oil

Herbs, Plants, Flowers
Pennyroyal, thyme, catnip, uva ursi, angelica, basil, burdock, yew, cypress, calendula

NOVEMBER MOON CORRESPONDENCES

November

Beaver Moon, Oak Moon, Frosty Moon, Mourning Moon, Tree Moon

It is called these names because beavers were caught and used to make warm articles of clothing for people. It was sometimes called the "Oak Moon" because it was named after the sacred oak tree, a tree that could successfully weather any winter storm.

INTENTION: TO PROTECT YOURSELF & YOUR LOVED ONES.

The November moon is a time for taking protective measures in you home and your life. Do cleansing rituals and set up some protective magic. Place crystals around your home and sprinkle a trail of salt around the edge of your property. Sew warm blankets, and crochet a scarf or hat for yourself and your loved ones. Quietly prepare.

Colors
A rich shade of green, cream, orange, gray, brown, white

Affirmation
"I use the power I hold to protect myself, my home, and my loved ones for any difficult time ahead. I trust the universe is good, and any pain leads to healing."

Crystals
Topaz, lapis lazuli, citrine, sodalite, bloodstone, yellow sapphire, obsidian, serpentine

Essential Oils
Cedar wood oil, cherry blossoms oil, hyacinth oil, peppermint oil, lemon oil

Herbs, Plants, Flowers
Blooming cacti, chrysanthemum, Venus flytrap, coriander, sage, rosemary

DECEMBER MOON CORRESPONDENCES

December
Cold Moon, Long Moon, Long Nights Moon, Oak Moon

It is called these names because during this moon, the nights are at their longest, and the temperatures are at their lowest. The winter solstice typically falls during this time.

INTENTION: TO CELEBRATE BIRTH, DEATH & TRANSFORMATION

The December moon is a time to draw close to your loved ones. Spread love to others, and give yourself love as well. Honor your desires that you've accomplished and meditate on the next phase of your life. Just as nature transforms each year, you will also transform.

Colors
Red, green, gold, white, silver, other metallic colors like brass or steel.

Affirmation

"I flow with the seasons. I open myself to the future. I allow time, nature, love, and the natural cycles of life to transform me. Everything is happening for me."

Crystals

Cherry quartz, clear quartz, amethyst, serpentine, jacinth, peridot, carnelian

Essential Oils

Violet oil, Patchouli oil, Rose Geranium oil, Frankincense oil, Myrrh oil, Lilac oil

Herbs, Plants, Flowers

Holly, poinsettia, Christmas cactus, English ivy, mistletoe, rose, pine, saffron, borage

CREATING YOUR OWN MONTHLY MOON CORRESPONDENCES

*A*ll that being said, the only reason those traditional monthly moon correspondences exist is because other witches who came before us created the traditions.

I personally believe that it's incredibly powerful to create your OWN traditions. I like to use lists of monthly correspondences as a jumping off point, but I always add my own personal touches based on what magical tools I have on hand and what my personal memories and associations are.

To create your own monthly moon names and correspondences, take a moment to journal about the following questions for each monthly moon.

- What is one treasured memory you have that occurred during this month/moon?
- What yearly activities happen in your life during this month/moon?
- What colors, emotions and moods do you associate with this month/moon?
- What holidays and traditions occur during this month/moon?

- What is the weather like during this month/moon?
- What is your favorite thing about this month/moon?

Next, look over your answers for each monthly moon and make some decisions. Have fun with this and don't overthink it! Overthinking is the enemy of witchcraft. Go with what your intuition tells you and don't judge yourself.

I love naming my moons for three reasons.

1. It creates a deep personal connection between me and the moon.

2. It's tied to my emotions. (Emotions are the secret sauce in magic.)

3. It helps me understand my personal priorities (and how they might differ from other witches).

Here's how I'd answer the journal prompts for my personal October Moon:

What is one treasured memory you have that occurred during this month/moon?
Healing from a breakup while watching eight seasons of Vampire Diaries.

What yearly activities happen in your life during this month/moon?
Staying inside more, pumpkin spice lattes and mulled wine, enjoying the leaves changing, carving pumpkins, kids in cute Halloween costumes.

What colors, emotions and moods do you associate with this month/moon?
Sadness, quietness, going inward, letting go of past hurt, being indulgent.

What holidays and traditions occur during this month/moon?

Halloween, lots of pumpkin bread baking, raking leaves, crock pot stews that make my apartment smell good all day.

What is the weather like during this month/moon?

Chilly, perfect Sweater weather! Also, it starts getting noticeably darker.

What is your favorite thing about this month/moon?

All the witchy vibes!

After looking over my answers, I'd say my dominant impression of the month of October is my treasured memory —healing my broken heart while watching the Vampire Diaries. Because of that, I could call the October moon my **Vampire Diaries Moon**.

If you've read my other books, you might already know this story, but for anyone who is just meeting me, here's why I'm so into the Vampire Diaries.

A couple years ago after I got my heart broken, I decided I was too depressed to do anything other than watch the entire Vampire Diaries series from beginning to end.

Every day for the whole month of October, I'd get myself a cup of tea and a slice of pumpkin bread, open up my laptop and click the Netflix play button. It didn't matter if it was a workday or a day off; I was glued to my MacBook screen, watching the misadventures of Damon, Elena and Stephen. (I worked at a really slow wine shop at the time and they let me watch Netflix and snack during my shift. It was a wonderful job.)

Silly as it sounds, Vampire Diaries was there for me when I was at one of my lowest moments. There was something really inspiring about watching the sensitive, troubled Damon Salvatore soldier on no matter how many times his heart got broken.

After this epic binge of vampire bad boys, I started to

feel the urge to do something with my life. My heartbreak slowly healed and my depression lifted. The day the credits rolled on the series finale, I was ready to get on with my life.

I immediately started outlining my paranormal cozy mystery novel, which became a five book series and opened my eyes to the creative and financial joys of self publishing. I owe all of that to the Vampire Diaries, and I think about that breakthrough every October.

Here are some ways I'd celebrate my Vampire Diaries moon based on my answers:

October Intention: I associate this moon with retreating from the world so I can regroup and rediscover who I am and what I want. October feels a bit melancholy because of my memories, but it also makes me feel excited for the possibilities that emerge after things fall apart. This is the energy of the Tower card in Tarot.

Colors: Orange and yellow (the colors of the leaves), black to represent the nights getting longer, dark red (the color of the Vampire Diaries logo).

Crystals: Onyx because it's black, labradorite because it's dreamy, smoky quartz because it helps release unwanted energy and emotions.

Essential Oils: Rose oil because roses cultivate love and forgiveness

Herbs/Plants/Flowers: Anything that smells like pumpkin bread (cinnamon, all-spice, ginger) and anything I add to my crock pot beef stew (sage, rosemary, and thyme). I might also put bay leaves on my October moon later because bay leaves represent luck. I feel so lucky that I was able to turn my heartbreak into a new career.

I would use all of these items when decorating my moon

altar and I'd incorporate them into my spells as much as possible during the entire October lunar cycle. Make sense?

The more you explore your own personal memories and traditions, the more confident you'll get with adding them to your moon practice. Just remember, there is no wrong answer here. There is no looking stupid. Whatever thoughts, feelings, and images that come up in your mind when you're thinking about the different moons is valid and meaningful. Often, that's how your intuition will speak to you!

PART IV

UNDERSTANDING THE ENERGY OF EACH MOON PHASE

WHAT ARE THE PHASES OF THE MOON + WHAT DO THEY MEAN?

*N*ow that you know the significance of the twelve (sometimes thirteen) monthly moons, let's get into the different phases within each lunar cycle.

It's important to note that not all witches observe the phases of the moon the same way.

There are actually four main ways witches choose to split up the lunar cycle.

As a secular (non-religion-based) witch, you are free to pick what moon cycle "system" you choose to live by. I switch between a two-phase and a four-phase system depending on how busy I am and what kind of magic I'm currently performing. The more phases you observe, the more complicated it gets, but as always, you do you!

System One: The Eight-Phase Lunar Cycle
New Moon
Crescent Waxing Moon
First Quarter Moon
Waxing Gibbous Moon
Full Moon

Waning Gibbous Moon
Third Quarter Moon
Waning Crescent Moon

System Two: The Nine-Phase Lunar Cycle

Some people use a nine-phase system to include the dark moon, which refers to the time in between the waning crescent moon and the new moon.

New Moon
Crescent Waxing Moon
First Quarter Moon
Waxing Gibbous Moon
Full Moon
Waning Gibbous Moon
Third Quarter Moon
Waning Crescent Moon
Dark Moon

System Three: The Four-Phase Lunar Cycle

This is the most common one I've seen, and one that fits in the best with my lifestyle.

New Moon
Waxing Moon
Full Moon
Waning Moon

System Four: The Two-Phase Lunar Cycle

If I've gotten off-track with my moon practice, I'll at least try to acknowledge when the new moon and the full moon roll around.

New Moon

Full Moon

One way isn't better than any of the others. Really. This isn't the time to beat yourself up for not remembering to cast a moon spell for all nine phases of the moon, every single month, until the end of time. I'm all about practical magic, and anything more than the four-phase cycle is too much for me. Does that make me a bad witch? No way. It's just how I choose to practice.

Other Powerful Lunar Times

There are other lunar events that happen throughout the year that super-charge any spells performed on those nights. If you see online or on the news that one of these special moons is occurring, consider carving out an evening to try casting more elaborate spells and manifesting one of your bigger goals.

Lunar Eclipse

A lunar eclipse happens when the sun, the earth and the moon are aligned. The earth completely blocks the sun from the moon, and the moon is completely inside the earth's shadow. The refracted light from the earth's atmosphere gives the moon a reddish hue. Unlike a solar eclipse, a lunar eclipse can be viewed without eye protection safely.

Perform any major releasing magic, such as cord-cutting, banishing energetic blocks, healing past heartbreak, and letting go of anything that you feel is holding you back.

Supermoon

A supermoon happens when the moon's orbit around the earth brings it close to the earth, making the moon appear larger than usual. This is basically a super-charged full moon. Cast your most far-fetched exciting spells on these nights.

Black Moon

Occasionally, there are two dark moon phases in a single month. The second dark moon phase is called the black moon. It's a time when our connection to the spiritual world is stronger. Any tarot readings, scrying, throwing bone readings, runes, psychic communication, spirit work, and seances will be super-charged with this special dark moon energy.

Blue Moon

There are two types of blue moons. One is a seasonal blue moon, which refers to the third full moon in a season with four full moons. This happens every 2 and a half years. The other blue moon is the second full moon in a month. Blue moons hold similar energy to a supermoon.

The Four Main Moon Phases

In this book, we'll focus on the four phase lunar cycle because it will get you an easy-to-follow, actionable overview of all the phases.

The New Moon

This moon phase can be honored for up to five days. This includes the 2 days before the new moon, the night of the new moon, and the two days after. During this phase, the moon will look totally dark and grow to a tiny sliver of light.

The energy of this moon is that of intention-setting. It's not typically a time for taking action. Think of it as a time of preparation, planning, and making adjustments. The new moon is a time for rest and quiet as you make lists and gather up everything you need for the projects, adventures, and rituals for the upcoming lunar cycle.

Things to do during this moon phase:

- Grocery shopping and meal prep
- Schedule appointments
- Write out your project or task schedule for the next cycle.
- Look back on the past lunar cycle and decide what you will change as you move forward.
- Rearrange your home.
- Have a heart to heart with your partner.
- Write out your goals for the month and check in with your goals for the year.
- Plan out what moon spells you'll do this month, and start putting together your lunar altar.
- Plan events, parties, or meetups with friends and loved ones for later this month.
- Consider making a new vision board, or editing an old vision board.
- Perform meditations that help you get clear on your priorities.
- Plant seeds during this phase.

How to celebrate this moon:

Hold a new moon ceremony. This can be with a group or

solo. It doesn't have to be anything crazy. Lighting some candles and meditating on your desires is a great way to celebrate the new moon. This is a time to plan and be still.

The Waxing Moon

This phase includes the Waxing Crescent Moon, the First Quarter Moon, and the Waxing Gibbous Moon.

This moon phase can be honored for about two weeks. This is the period of time between the new moon phase and the full moon phase. During the waxing moon phase, the moon will go from a tiny sliver to almost a full moon. Every night, it will appear a bit bigger and brighter.

The energy of the waxing moon is that of action and growth. Think about anything you want to add, grow, increase or achieve in your life, and take as much action as possible during this phase to manifest your desires.

Things to do during this moon phase:

- If you are getting any surgery that is "adding" to your body like a hip or knee replacement, or any kind of implant, you can schedule it for this moon phase.
- Plan any product launches or money-making ventures during this time.
- Add things to your home, your closet, or your appearance during this time.
- Grow plants.
- Create things.
- Make craft projects.
- Make art.
- Sign up for a class to learn a new skill.
- Focus on adding things to your routine.

- If you are working on improving your physical body, work on adding muscle with strength training rather than losing fat.

How to celebrate this moon:

Take action and use the momentum to make progress towards your desires. You can charge water in waxing moon energy. Drinking waxing-moon-charged water will increase your energy. This is great for drinking hard workouts at the gym or sipping during a late night study session. This water is also fantastic to use when watering your plants. Try performing a few moon bath meditations in this energy as well and journal about how the energy affects your mood.

The Full Moon

This moon phase can be celebrated for about five days. This includes the two days before the full moon, the night of the full moon, and the two days following the full moon. The moon will appear as a big, bright ball of light. During this time, the moon is at its largest and brightest!

Full moon energy is potent, and it can sometimes feel a bit too powerful. It is a time for manifesting and celebrating. If you have been feeling stuck, any action you take during the full moon will help you get unstuck.

Things to do during this moon phase:

- Dance under the full moon.
- Perform a moon bath meditation in this highly charged energy.
- Do things that require luck during this moon phase.

- Do not schedule any dental or medical procedures.
- Use this time to be around family and friends if that feels good. The full moon is a very social time.
- If being social feels overwhelming, find a way to celebrate the full moon alone.
- Do something indulgent during this phase, like getting your hair done, getting a massage or a manicure.
- Make a big dinner or go out to eat.
- Harvest herbs and make herb bundles.
- Cleanse magical tools, water, and yourself in the energy of the full moon.
- Eat something sweet and decadent like chocolate-covered strawberries.
- Have a glass of wine or hot chocolate if that is something you enjoy.

How to celebrate this moon phase

Host a full moon ceremony, also known as an esbat. During your ceremony, cast spells in front of your altar with all the traditional or personal correspondences you associated with that month's full moon. Decorate your home with fresh flowers and light candles. Take a ritual bath with oils, crystals, flower petals and pink sea salt. Write out your intentions and burn them in a fireproof container under the light of the full moon. Practice divination during this time.

The Waning Moon

This phase includes the waning Gibbous Moon, Third Quarter Moon, and Waning Crescent Moon.

This moon phase lasts for about two weeks. This phase goes from the end of the full moon to the beginning of the new moon. The moon will appear to decrease in size and brightness each night. The moon will start out large and "shrink" to a tiny sliver of light.

The energy of the waning moon is that of releasing and letting go.

Things to do during this moon phase:

- Intentions like weight loss and decreasing debt are perfect for this moon phase.
- Take time to be alone and try to mediate each day during this phase.
- You might feel a bit more irritable than usual and that's OK!
- Rest more, and if you don't feel like doing something, plan to skip it during this moon phase.
- If you want to work out, consider a restful walk, a yoga class, or a stretching class.

How to celebrate this moon:

Listen to your body, your mind, your emotions, and your spirit. Say no if you do not have the energy. Practice self care as often as possible. If you have children, consider getting child care or a babysitter for some of the days during this moon phase. See a movie, binge watch Netflix, be lazy. If you feel called to do a ritual, try candle gazing, a ritual bath, or journaling. Burn incense and drink lots of tea.

The Dark Moon can either be included in the new moon phase or the waning moon phase. This is a time for planning AND letting things fall away. Be still and try to connect with your intuition or your higher power (or spirit guides) during this time. You will hear the answers as clearly as ever during this magical phase.

Some witches choose to do absolutely nothing on the night of the dark moon. They don't cook. They don't work. They kick up their feet and relax, and they don't feel the least bit guilty about it. If you feel stressed out, try meditating under the dark moon. As someone prone to anxiety, I find it incredibly calming.

NEW MOON SPELLS

Crystal Lavender Wine Ritual

This beautiful and magical wine elixir is perfect for a new moon. Have a cup of this as you sit outside and gaze at the moon, or get cozy in your home, sitting by a window. The soothing effects of the lavender quiet your mind and spirit, while the citrine crystal will get your creative juices flowing.

Drinking a cup of this will open your mind to new possibilities in your life. Enjoy alone on a quiet evening, or with a group of your besties.

What You'll Need

- A glass of white wine (riesling works well for this)
- A funnel
- A tumbled citrine crystal
- Edible dried lavender edible

Directions

On the eve of the New Moon, open the bottle of white wine. Pour a bit of wine in a glass, so the bottle isn't totally full. Use a funnel to drop about ½ teaspoon of dried lavender buds into the bottle.

> Note: Make sure your lavender buds are free of pesticides or chemicals and are safe to eat. If you don't have lavender in your garden, check out your local farmer's market or specialty grocery store for edible flowers. Double check with the seller that the flowers are safe to eat. You can also find edible flowers online.

Speak your intention aloud, or in your mind as you do this. Create your own or use this one: "With this lavender, I call on the element of earth to quiet my mind and ground me as the new moon approaches."

Use the funnel to pour the wine back into the bottle. If it all doesn't fit with room for the cork, go ahead and drink the last bit from your cup. Seal the bottle with the cork and refrigerate the wine.

On the night of the new moon, take the bottle of wine out of the fridge and pour yourself a glass. Use a mesh sieve to remove the lavender. It is now infused with the wine. As you do this, speak your intention aloud or in your mind. Create your own or use this one: "With this wine, I call on the element of water to strengthen my connection to my intuition. May I hear the wisdom it has to offer."

Place the tumbled piece of citrine into the glass of wine. The orange-yellow color of the citrine is sometimes associated with fire. Allow five minutes for the crystal's energy to transfer into the liquid. Say aloud or in your mind an intention. You can make up your own or use this one: "With this citrine crystal, I call on the power of fire. Send me a bright idea on this night of the full moon."

> Note: Make sure you thoroughly wash your crystal, and that it doesn't have any cracks in it.

Remove the crystal with a piece of silverware, and sip your wine. Do anything you like as you sip your wine—meditate, read, watch tv, chat with friends—whatever. If any new insights occur to you, be sure to write them down.

Herb Bundle New Moon Ritual

What You'll Need

- An assortment of fresh herbs
- Strips of paper
- Baker's Twine
- Scissors
- Flower petals (optional)

Directions

1. Cut your herbs so they are about six inches long.
2. Cut your string so it is about three times that length (18 inches long in this case).
3. Write one intention on each sheet of paper.
4. Gather the herbs and flower petals up in a small bouquet, tucking one strip of paper into each bouquet.
5. Tie a knot at the bottom of the herb bundle and wind the string up and down until everything is secure.
6. Tie another knot at the bottom to complete your bundle.

Leave these to dry in the sun, or cover them with paper towels and put them in the microwave for a minute or two.

Burn these bundles on the night of the full moon as you meditate on your goals, desires, and achievements that you set during the previous new moon.

WAXING MOON SPELLS

Planting Intentions Waxing Moon Spell

Perform this spell on any night during the waxing moon. It's perfect for any intention that involves growing something or increasing something (such as your bank account)!

What You'll Need

- A garden, or a pot and soil
- Any kind of seeds
- A small piece of paper
- A jar of water that has sat in the waxing moonlight for at least one night

Write down something you want to increase or manifest during the next week. Bury the paper in the soil with a seed. Water the soil with water charged with the energy of the waxing moon. Know that your intentions are manifesting just as the seed is growing. Trust that nature is bringing you the growth and abundance you desire.

Waxing Moon Money Milk Bath

This bath spell is perfect for calling in abundance, particularly in the form of some fast cash.

What You'll Need

- One teaspoon of nutmeg
- One teaspoon of cinnamon
- One tablespoon of dried mint
- ½ cup of cornstarch
- 2 cups of milk powder
- ½ cup baking soda
- A clear quartz crystal
- A clean coin
- Green candles
- A mason jar or any jar with an airtight lid

Directions

Pour all the ingredients into a mason jar. Shake up the mixture. Drop a clear quartz crystal and a clean coin into the mixture and seal up. Place the jar near a window or outside for one night to soak up the waxing moon energy.

When you are ready for your bath, remove the coin and the crystal. Pour a ½ cup or so of the mixture in running water as you're filling your bath. Light green candles and enjoy your decadent money milk bath.

FULL MOON SPELLS

Full Moon Mirror Spell

What You'll Need
A handheld mirror

On the night of the full moon, go outside and find somewhere you can see the full moon. Greet the full moon and take a moment to soak in its potent energy. Position your mirror so it is catching the moon and reflecting it towards you.

Stand there and absorb the glow. This energy will enhance your physical appearance, increase confidence, wash away unwanted energy, and fill you with love. When you feel complete, thank the moon and go inside. For the rest of the lunar cycle, your mirror will retain the full moon's beauty-enhancing energy. Whenever you desire that energy, simply gaze into the mirror to absorb it.

Full Moon Pink Love Bath

What You'll Need

- A handful of rose petals
- ½ cup pink Himalayan sea salt
- ½ cup baking soda
- One teaspoon of dried lavender
- Two drops of orange essential oil (Check with a doctor before using any essential oil. This stuff is potent.)
- ½ cup of red wine
- Your most romantic music playlist
- Two white candles, tea lights are perfect

Turn on your playlist and light your candles. Set your intention for this spell. Because it is the full moon, a celebratory intention will be most powerful. Create your own or use this one: "Full moon, I celebrate all the love I've manifested in my life. Love surrounds me like water."

You can specify what kind of love you are manifesting with the full moon—a new romantic relationship, healing a current relationship, self-love, strengthening the bonds of friendship, or anything else you want.

Run your bath water and add your ingredients one at a time in whatever order you want. As you add each one, meditate on one way you already have abundant love in your life, such as the love of your parents, the love of your dog, the love from the moon, or the love you give to yourself.

Step into the bath and visualize a scene between you and the ideal person you are performing the spell for. See yourself and your person in your mind's eye sitting down at a beautiful restaurant. Enjoy the dinner conversation and the interaction you two create. Allow yourself to get lost in it.

When you feel complete, you can get out of the bath.

Trust that the moon is already co-creating your desired relationship, and sending it towards you.

WANING MOON SPELLS

Waning Moon Forgiveness Ritual
Hawaiian meditation: "ho'oponopono"

Perform this ritual on the night of the waning moon (or whenever you need to release and forgive.

What You'll Need

- A purple candle
- A bundle of herb (sage works great for this)
- A small fireproof container or a cauldron
- A journal

*P*erform this ritual on the night of the waning moon (or whenever you need to release and forgive.

Directions

Light a purple candle and use that flame to light your

dried herb bundle. Walk and the candle to create a sacred circle. This is your safe place to get vulnerable and honest with yourself. Say aloud or in your head, "I call on the power of the waning moon to help me shed my false beliefs so I may heal my emotional wounds."

Set the smoking herb bundle in your fireproof container. Sit in front of the candle and herb bundle.

Begin meditating or journaling.

Think about or journal about a moment or situation that made you feel bad or lowered your vibration. Get as detailed as you want with it. You know you've hit on the issue when you feel a rush of emotion as you write.

Close your eyes and allow yourself to mentally "travel back" to that moment. See the person who wronged you. Allow the full extent of the pain to wash over you. Look the person in the eyes and say (either aloud or in your head):

"I love you. I'm sorry. Please forgive me. Thank you."

Say (or think) each sentence slowly. Know that you're doing this ritual for your own spiritual growth and healing. That can help release some of the pain. Even if you don't have any positive feelings for the person who hurt you, focus on the healing you will receive as a result of you being brave enough to perform this ritual.

Here's how you can think about each sentence in this ritual:

"I love you." I acknowledge the love I have for this person because I recognize my connection to every living being on this earth. I choose love even in the face of pain.

"I'm sorry." I'm sorry for the part I played in this pain. I'm sorry for the hurt I caused you. I'm sorry that you did what you did. I'm sorry I went through that experience. I acknowledge the deep pain that came from this experience.

Note: even if this experience was not your fault AT ALL, by apologizing, you are taking back your power and stepping into it fully—not giving it away.

"Please forgive me." Forgive me for the role I played. Again, even if you've done nothing wrong, the ritual of saying this will facilitate deep release and healing.

"Thank you." Thank you for being present in this ritual. Thank you for participating. Thank you for being a part of my spiritual journey and spiritual healing.

Repeat these phrases (aloud or in your head) until you feel the pain begin to loosen and leave your body. You may have to repeat this ritual several times before you feel the release.

Waning Moon Water Spell

Perform this simple spell when you have some kind of negative energy you'd like to release.

What You'll Need
A cup of hot or cold water

Go outside or by a window to absorb the releasing energy of the waning moon. Hold the cup of water in both hands. Use hot water if your negative emotion is making you angry, frustrated, resentful, or jealous. Use cold water if your energy feels sad, lonely, ashamed, or scared. If your energy is a combination, just pick whichever temperature feels right. Close your eyes and allow your hands to feel the temperature of the water through the glass. Energetically connect to the water. Say aloud or in your head the energy you'd like to release.

Visualize that energy moving out into your arms, into your hands and getting absorbed in the water. You can visualize this energy as a color, a light, or anything you want. If any emotions come up as you do this, let them move through you and into the water. Don't judge or hold on to anything.

When you feel like the energy has released, pour the water out in a sink or outside. Know that the unwanted energy is out of you and flowing away with the water. If you still feel upset, that's ok. Trust that the farther away that water goes, the better you will feel. Thank the moon for helping you with your spell.

MOON PHASE ENERGETIC AFFIRMATIONS

New Moon
I see my goals clearly and feel the job as if it has already manifested.

Waxing Crescent Moon
I create a plan of action to draw my goals to myself.

First Quarter Moon
I move towards my goals with courage and creativity.

Waxing Gibbous Moon
My power is perfectly aligned with the universe.

Full Moon
Now is the time. I am unstoppable.

Waning Gibbous Moon
I celebrate all I have accomplished.

Third Quarter Moon

Everyday I get wiser and I make positive changes in my life.

Waning Crescent Moon
I let go of the past and understand that mistakes are opportunities for growth.

Dark Moon
I rest in the knowledge that all is well. Everything happens in the right way, at the right time.

MENSTRUAL CYCLES + THE MOON

Historically, women's menstrual cycles were believed to follow the cycles of the moon. As witchcraft and spirituality become more mainstream, more women are curious about the connection between their bodies and lunar energy.

A typical menstrual cycle lasts about 28 days and a complete moon cycle goes for 29.5 days. Though they don't match up perfectly, it's pretty close.

If you're a witch who is interested in learning how and why some people track their menstrual cycle along with the moon, this chapter is for you!

If this isn't your cup of tea, no worries. You can skip this chapter and not miss out on anything of the magic.

Your Period and the Moon

Centuries ago, before electricity, cell phone screens, airplane travel, and a lot of other really cool technological advances, many women's periods were synched up with the moon.

In general, the majority of women ovulated during the full moon, and bled during the new moon.

Back then, people often lived in close proximity to each other.

If you've ever gone to summer camp or lived on a college campus with a bunch of menstruating women, you might have experienced this "syncing" phenomenon.

At the risk of giving you T.M.I, I've had this happen to me when I was living with about fifteen other women in a remote community in Alaska. We all got our periods at the same time, and together, we went through all the different moods and energies that happen in a woman's cycle.

In some Native American cultures, women took part in a gathering sometimes called a "Red Tent Ceremony". Women would retreat from their usual routines and hang out with each other—talking, resting, and bonding until their periods were over.

These women celebrated the cycle of menstruation, knowing that it brought new life into the world. Women's menstrual blood was considered sacred and was associated with power, the ability to create, and abundance.

I've never had a baby, but I would say that birthing seems to be a powerful act of manifesting.

In those same communities that held "Red Tent Ceremonies", there were several women who bled during the full moon and ovulated during the new moon. These women were believed to be healers, creatives, artists, spiritual leaders, and priestesses.

The Mother, the Maiden, and the Crone

The **triple moon symbol** is a well-recognized symbol in the magical community. It shows the moon in three phases, side-by-side-the waxing moon on the left, the full moon in the middle and the waning moon on the right.

Magical tradition teaches the idea that these three lunar cycles represent different phases in a woman's life cycle—**the mother, the maiden, and the crone.**

The waxing moon is the maiden. This represents women before she begins her menstrual cycle. It is a time for exploration, growth, movement, and carefree innocence.

The full moon is the mother. This represents a woman during the time in her life when she gets her period. She is fertile, able to give birth, create, and nurture. This is a time of celebration, harvest, and enjoying all that you have created with your beautiful, sensual, feminine power.

The waning moon is the crone. This phase represents a woman after she's gone into menopause. Historically, the crone is known as a wise woman, a healer, a leader in her community, a woman who people went to for guidance, mentorship, and encouragement. This is a time for going inward, resting, and embracing the strong connection you have to the spiritual world.

Each of these phases holds great power. Each of these is a significant milestone in a woman's life.

The Mother, the Maiden, and the Crone in Fairy Tale Tropes

OK, I'm going to vent for a second about how women—particularly magic-minded women—are sometimes put in a (rather unflattering) box.

There are certain words used in the magical community that are misunderstood by today's society. The word "witch" brings up images of an evil old woman covered in worts with a pointy nose who stirs a cauldron and cackles about all the curses she's going to put on poor unsuspecting fair maidens.

Shakespeare's Macbeth coined the famous witchy phrase, "Double, double, toil and trouble…"

And that's just the beginning of the misguided references to witches and their magical practice.

Think about that for a second.

A common trope in fairy tales and folklore is the old, ugly witch (the crone) putting a curse on the maiden.

What is that teaching us?

That maidens aren't powerful.

That they're helpless and naïve and need protecting from the evil in the world.

That a maiden's only asset is her youth and innocence.

This says nothing of what maidens are really like—girls, teenagers, or young women who thirst for adventure, knowledge, who take risks, make mistakes, and explore life with passion and drive.

The crone in this fairytale trope is a powerful woman, but she's using that power for evil. Usually, she's depicted as an old woman who longs to get back the beauty of her youth that she's lost. She's feared, but she's not respected. She's wise, but no person with good intentions would ever seek her guidance.

Again, it all goes back to the idea that beauty equals a woman's value, which isn't true.

Women are meant to be celebrated, not because they are beautiful, not because they are wise, not even because they can give birth.

Women should be celebrated because they ARE.

Women (and those who identify as women) are beautiful, wise, wild, sensual, and intuitive. They bring something unique when they come into this world. They interact with others, and they heal through being their authentic, messy selves.

That is where a woman's value comes from.

Simply being.
So take that, sexist fairy tale trope!

Do Women Need To Be Mothers?

The "mother" in the moon tradition is represented by the full moon. Women in society are often expected to be mothers, and if they're not, they may face judgment or at the very least, confusion from other people. Women without children are sometimes viewed as "less than".

This is another false belief that we've learned from society. I believe that women aren't obligated to have children, and they certainly aren't less than because of that. Women can "create" in more ways than giving birth. Creation comes in the form of creating a life for herself, creating joy, creating a business, creating art, or creating healings. The fertile energy of the full moon extends to anything a woman wants to create or pursue.

At the same time, women who are mothers are sometimes expected to give up on themselves and their own self-care to raise their children. But by doing that, a woman is not honoring herself, and actually not even honoring the people she cares for because how can she show up as her best self when she is constantly tired, resentful, or stressed? Sometimes a mother is expected to "do it all" by being both a mother and have a career. And yes, sometimes women are resourceful enough to figure it out, but being able to (or having the desire to) "do it all" does not add to or take away from a woman's value.

If you identify as a woman and this aspect of moon magic appeals to you, think about your role as a woman every time the moon moves into your current phase: maiden, mother, or crone. Celebrate your value and your unique energy no matter what phase of life you are in.

How to Align Your Menstrual Cycle to the Moon

Part of the reason why the full moon is associated with fertility is because long ago, women's menstrual cycles synced to the lunar cycles.

The reason a woman's period syncs to the moon cycles is actually because of the amount of light that a woman is exposed to overnight and her menstrual cycle. Light stimulates the pituitary gland, which causes ovulation.

This makes sense because the moon gives off a different amount of light each night depending on what phase the moon is in.

If you wanted to try syncing your cycle to the moon, that way you would do that is to control the amount of light that you're exposed to once the sun goes down.

Here's a breakdown of the days of the lunar cycle:

- Days 1-6 Menstruation (New Moon)
- Days 7-13 Pre-ovulation (Waxing Moon)
- Days 14-21 Ovulation (Full Moon)
- Days 22-28 Pre-menstruation (Waning Moon)

Ways to Sync Your Period to the Moon

- Limit the time you spend on your laptop, TV or phone after the sun goes down.
- If you sleep by a large window (in a place with little light pollution outside), turn off all the lights when you sleep and keep the window open.
- Sleep with a 100-watt light bulb on during the five nights of the full moon.

- Sit outside under the moon as often as possible, particularly during the full moon.
- Keep your house in tune with the night sky. If it's light outside, keep it light inside, and vice versa.
- Use candlelight as much as possible after the sun goes down.

Some of these practices might work for you. Others might be totally impractical. Try what works for you and discard the rest.

Why You Shouldn't Stress About Aligning Your Cycle to the Moon

The most important thing is for you to be healthy! If your period is regular, no matter when you ovulate, that's wonderful! That is your own personal full moon.

You do not have to be in sync with the moon. You are not "more magical" or "more aligned" if your period matches the moon phases. You are in alignment when you honor your own cycles. Don't force your body into something that doesn't feel natural. Follow your own rhythms.

You can experiment with different light therapy methods and see if your menstrual cycle changes over time, but seriously, don't stress about it.

PART V

MOON MAGIC FUNDAMENTALS

HOW TO WRITE + CAST YOUR OWN MOON SPELL

I love performing spells created and perfected by others. I have several books and one huge grimoire of spells that I routinely go to for inspiration and ideas for magic. If you're curious about the big grimoire I use, it's called The Encyclopedia of 5,000 Spells by Judika Illes. You can get your own copy if you head over to www.whitewitchacademy.com/resources.

That being said, I believe that intention and emotion are the most important parts of any spell.

For your spell to be effective, you must align your mind, body, and emotions to your intention. Every time I have done this—and addressed any limiting beliefs or blocks or attachments that come up—I have seen results from my magic.

Sometimes the result is not exactly what I expected, but it has always been positive. Sometimes it takes a few weeks or even months, but it usually comes.

There is science coming out in the field of quantum mechanics that shows evidence for why magic works.

You can read more about this in *Breaking the Habit of*

Being Yourself, by Dr. Joe Dispenza. It covers topics on manifesting and how to heal negative thought patterns, and yes, some fascinating scientific theories to back up the principle of manifesting.

I won't get into the details here, but to make this extremely simplistic, there's something called the "Observer Effect" where an electron, one of the smallest parts of an atom, would move randomly UNLESS someone was observing it. Then the electron would show up wherever the observer was looking. The theory behind this is that your mind is controlling the electron. You're manifesting it. You're using your inner power to manipulate that subatomic particle.

I bring that up to hopefully get you more open to the idea of writing and performing your own spells. I believe that 100 years from now, people will be talking about manifesting (and magic) in mainstream education. Once science catches up with the spiritual world, everyone's going to be embracing their inner power.

In the meantime, you can use these principles to create magic in your own life.

Here's how to write and cast an effective moon spell:

Step One: Figure out what you want.

There are a lot of ways to do this and we've talked about this in previous lessons, but here's one way I use often.

Set a timer for ten minutes. Write furiously and continuously about your ideal life until the timer goes off. Don't stop writing until you hear the alarm. Even if you're just writing "I don't know what to write", just keep on writing until something starts to rise up out of your subconscious.

Step Two: Read over your writing and pick out one

thing in your "ideal life vision" that gets you really excited today.

This might change tomorrow, or next week, so just focus on what is exciting to you today. Also, don't try to manifest all of these things in one spell.

Pick one thing that you really want. This can be an actual thing like a car or a home. Or it can be a job, money, or calling in a romantic love, etc. It can be a bit abstract, like "releasing anger".

Step Three: Distill that "thing" into one or two powerful sentences.

Let's say I chose to "release the anger I hold" towards a person in my life. To turn this into a spell, you can change the focus to the positive, not the negative. Then make that statement in the present tense and first person.

Instead of: "I release my anger towards Sarah."

Change it to: "I feel a rush of love when I see Sarah."

So now the focus is on calling in love, not releasing anger, even though, essentially, it's the same thing.

Step Four: Gather up any items that hold magical or personal significance.

This can involve herbs, colors, candles, photos, magazine images, and whatever you think will support your intention.

Remember to get items that will do one of three things:

- Help you focus mentally on your intention (aligned thoughts)
- Call up strong emotion (aligned feelings)
- Connect you to your intention physically (aligned body)

I would use a photo of Sarah, probably a picture from her Facebook, that I pulled up on my phone. I'd set that right up on my altar. This would help me focus my thoughts on Sarah.

I'd also use an herb bundle with dried thyme and pink rose petals because I find the smell very calming, and it will help my heart to open up. Pink rose petals make me feel loving, warm fuzzies which will support my intention of cultivating love for Sarah. The herb bundle of thyme and rose petals will satisfy the aligned body and feeling requirements.

Step Five: Decide how long you want to do this spell and what time of day.

Spells work mainly from our subconscious mind when your brain is putting out alpha or theta brain waves. Basically, we are usually in beta brain wave mode, and alpha is one step slower. You can think of theta as two steps slower. When your brain is in theta, you're in a state of deep meditation while still being awake.

A spell performed when your brain is in alpha or theta states will be super-charged.

To allow enough time for your brain to slip into alpha or theta, put aside at least ten minutes for your magic. If you have time, consider lengthening your spell to thirty or forty-five minutes.

As for time of day, you are most likely to slip into these states of awareness first thing in the morning or right before bed.

It doesn't matter which you pick, and keep in mind that if early morning or late at night doesn't work with your schedule, that's OK. Find a time that works with your life. Regardless of the time of day you perform your spell, you will still be able to use the moon's energy.

Step Six: Sink into your visualization and let the outside world fade away.

This, as they say, is where the magic happens. Gaze at the

focal point on your altar, or close your eyes as you start to visualize your specific intention.

For my spell, I will begin by visualizing a scene where I'm looking at Sarah and seeing her smile at me. Maybe I'll step towards her and hold out my hand to shake, and she'll surprise me by pulling me into a hug.

Continue to gently guide any wandering thoughts back to the focus of your spell by visualizing your specific scene or gazing at the focal point on your altar.

Notice where in your body you feel the intention resonating. Do you feel it in your chest? Your stomach? What does it feel like? Butterflies in your stomach? A warmth in your chest? Does it make your heart speed up? Does it make your cheeks heat up? Do you feel any lightheadedness? Notice all of these physical sensations.

Pay attention to emotions that surface as you meditate. Name them as they rise up from deep within you. It doesn't matter if the emotions are good or bad. While you are meditating, simply experience the feelings, then name them, and allow them to pass through you.

That is how you align all three parts of you to make your spell as powerful as possible.

Step Seven: Complete your spell.

To do this, deepen your breath, open your eyes, and say thank you to the moon, the universe, and yourself for co-creating.

HOW TO CREATE A POWERFUL ALTAR

One of my favorite parts of moon magic is creating moon altars.

If you don't believe me, check out my Instagram (@whitewitchacademy). I have many pictures of my monthly moon-themed altars.

The concept of an altar might bring up all kinds of images and ideas. I have a religious background, so I associated an altar with a big table positioned in the front of a church.

In secular witchcraft, an altar is a bit different. It's highly personal and incredibly versatile. No two altars are the same!

Your altars will probably change as you change. You might add additional items to your altar as the moon moves phases or as the seasons shift. Maybe you change it depending on what day of the week it is.

It doesn't matter what you want your altar to look like, but there are two guidelines to keep in mind as you're deciding how you'd like to set up your altar.

- Location and type of altar
- Purpose of your altar

Location and Type of Altar

Where do you want your altar to be?

This comes down to your lifestyle and living situation. If you live alone or with people who are supportive of your magical practice, you can have a permanent space in your home where you meditate and perform your magic.

If you go this route, you can find a quiet place in your home like a sunroom, a corner in your bedroom, a sitting room, even a place in your garage. You can set up a table or platform of some kind and place your altar cloth and magical items on top of your altar. Maybe this space is a windowsill that you arrange your objects along.

You'll want a place to sit so that you're comfortable when you're at your altar. This can be a pillow, a yoga bolster, a stool, a chair, etc. Pick something that you know you'll be OK with sitting in for an extended period of time. You don't want to have to end your spell because your knees are hurting!

If you love to change up your altar and put different things on it depending on your purpose or mood, keep a box nearby and place your magical objects inside when you're not using them. This is especially important if you have a lot of fragile objects, like thin candles or crystals. I've definitely damaged my magical items before by shoving them haphazardly in a drawer because I didn't have a dedicated place for them.

If you live in a place where you don't feel comfortable having a permanent altar in your home, you can create a portable altar.

Use a box, a tote bag, a pencil case, or a drawer as your altar. Simply take out whatever objects you need for the spell you're doing, set them up, perform the spell, and put everything away.

Remember, an altar is meant to support your lifestyle, not interrupt it. Don't let anyone tell you differently. Magic is practical and versatile, not rigid and pretentious.

Another thing to consider when picking a location for your altar is privacy. Is that something you value? If so, you might want to make sure you have your altar somewhere with a door and a lock.

Maybe that means having your altar in your closet, your attic, your bathroom, or a private outdoor location. You want to feel totally yourself without judgment or anxiety about what others think.

The most important thing is that the location of your altar needs to feel good. The energy of that space should relax you and get you in the mood for magic. You should feel safe when you are sitting in front of your altar.

Purpose of Your Altar

The purpose of your altar can remain the same for years, or you can change it up each time you sit down to practice magic.

Altar Themes and Intentions:

You can pick a theme or intention for your altar as you're setting it up. You can go general such as "celebrating nature", "honoring the moon", or "connecting to your inner power". Conversely, you can get more specific, such as manifesting a job, banishing a negative thought pattern, or calling in a soul mate.

If you're creating an altar based on the energy of the current monthly moon, decorate it with traditional colors, herbs, crystals, and whatever flowers are in season. As I mentioned before, don't be afraid to create your own moon correspondences, too!

What to Put On Your Altar

Be sure to pick items to place on your altar that hold personal significance to you that support your intention.

For example: if you're setting up an altar to call in a soulmate, you can put items on the altar that make you feel emotions that you associate with love and romance. This could include a movie stub from a romantic date that made you so happy, a postcard of your dream wedding destination, or a bottle of nail polish that makes you feel sexy.

An item is appropriate for your altar if it:

- makes you feel a strong positive emotion
- makes you think of a strong positive memory
- helps you focus on your intention

If you've placed items on your altar that make you feel a bit sad, consider either doing shadow work to heal that resistance or remove the item from your altar.

For example, if the movie ticket stub made you sad because it reminds you of a time when you felt romantic love, but also makes you aware of how lonely you are currently, that's not going to be the best energy to perform magic with.

You can choose to replace the item with something else, like your favorite novel with a love story that resonated with you.

Mental Altars

If you don't want to do a physical altar, you can do a mental altar. All you need is to close your eyes and visualize an altar. Your altar can have anything on it, and it can be in any location.

In your mind's eye, you can have an altar covered with huge shiny crystals, vibrant flower petals, and golden candelabras. Your altar can be in an old, romantic castle in Scotland, in the tranquil jungles of Bali, or even on a space ship soaking through the galaxy.

Multiple studies have proven that your brain does not differentiate between a real experience and an imagined experience. Because of that, this extravagant imaginary altar can actually help you manifest things like financial abundance and exotic travel.

If you feel like a person who just got done touring a castle in Scotland, you will begin attracting that experience into your physical reality.

So this brings me to the next point. Which is that magic WORKS. Here's why:

Why Altars Work

Altars are so, SO good for manifesting and performing magic. The reason for this is they combine ALL of the necessary elements of manifesting.

The three necessary elements are:

- Clear intention
- Heightened emotion
- Connection to the physical realm

The objects on your altar help you focus on exactly what you are trying to accomplish with your magic. The objects you've chosen also have personal significance to you, which will heighten the desired emotions whenever you sit in front of that altar.

There's research that suggests that our brains respond to images and visualizations. When we look at an altar (whether it's with our eyes or with our mind's eye) we activate the neural transmitters in our bodies, connecting the brain to the body, and that alignment is exactly what you need to begin the manifesting process.

PART VI

MOON + MAGICAL TOOLS CHEAT SHEETS

CRYSTALS BY MOON PHASE

Moonstone
Strengthens intuition, connects you to the moon and the universe, spiritual awareness, safe travel, shadow work (banishing wounds, blocks, and limiting beliefs), and protection.

Uses:
Hold while meditating, use as a focal point on a crystal grid (carved as a skull for a spiritual awareness crystal grid, a crystal point to send a specific intention directly to the moon, or as a sphere shape to represent the moon itself.) Don't place this stone in water.

Moon Phase:
Any moon phase, but its energy most closely matches the new moon and the waning moon phases.

Selenite

Mental clarity, heightened psychic abilities, deep meditation, putting big new moon intentions into play.

Uses:

Hold this while meditating or using tarot cards (or any kind of divination work), touch it to different places on your body to release energetic blocks and physical tension. Don't place this stone in water.

Moon Phase:

New moon and full moon phases.

∼

Labradorite

Promotes good sleep habits, gives you insightful dreams, connects you to the spirit world, increases intuitive abilities, powers any magic you perform in the evening hours.

Uses:

Place four of these crystals in a square shape on your crystal grid or altar to give you protection while you open your heart to the energy of the spirit world, place it under your pillow for a restful sleep, light a candle and watch the flame light up the brilliant blue-green colors of this stone as you perform candle spells. Don't place this stone in water.

Moon Phase:

Waning moon

∼

Clear Quartz

Amplifies any positive energy or intention in magic.

Uses:
Place a circle of clear quartz on an altar or crystal grid, use in a ritual bath, make a crystal elixir by placing a piece of washed, tumbled clear quartz in a beverage such as kombucha, tea, or water. (This crystal is safe to place in water, but avoid extreme temperatures.) Carry this crystal in your pocket for an extra dose of manifesting power and positivity.

Moon Phase:
All of them, but its energy matches the new moon, the waxing moon, and the full moon energies the most.

∼

Carnelian
Enhances creativity, increases motivation, attracts a lover who connects with you on a spiritual level, increases passion, helps generate good ideas, determination, resilience, and endurance.

Uses:
A great crystal for elixirs (almond milk, kombucha, tea, coffee, or water), use as a focal point on a love crystal grid, hold while you meditate, carry with you in your pocket to help bring you good ideas and creative inspiration. Use in a ritual bath with jasmine oil and rose petals to call in a lover, or combine carnelian with citrine and basil for a success and abundance ritual bath. (This crystal is safe to place in water, but avoid extreme temperatures.)

Moon Phase:

Full moon

~

Blue Apatite
Helps with communication, gives you courage to speak your truth, helps you manifest your big goals, helps you get clear on what you really want and gives you energy to take inspired action.

Uses:
Charge your waxing moon water with this stone before diffusing it with lemon oil and peppermint oil, meditate while holding this stone before a difficult conversation or a public speaking engagement, sleep with it near your bed or under your pillow to help your subconscious work on manifesting your desires while you sleep. (This crystal is safe to place in water, but avoid extreme temperatures.)

Moon Phase:
Waxing moon

~

Amethyst
Emotional healing, releasing negative energy, helps break unwanted habits, holds calming and balancing energy, increases spiritual awareness.

Uses:
Place amethyst stones on a crystal grid with clear quartz and labradorite and allow the energy of the grid to cleanse a space and charge it with heightened spiritual awareness. Perform divination like tarot or scrying in that space. Charge water

with this stone when you are introducing new habits into your life and sip the water all day to soak up the benefits of this crystal. Use with sprigs of lavender, oatmeal, sea salt and amethyst for a shadow work waning moon bath ritual. As you soak in the tub, visualize the unwanted energy, limiting beliefs, and blocks rising out of your body. (This crystal is safe to place in water, but avoid extreme temperatures.)

Moon Phase:
Full moon or waning moon.

Citrine
Success, financial abundance, good business, love, positivity, confidence, and good ideas.

Uses:
Create a crystal grid with citrine, pyrite and aventurine for a financial abundance ritual, place in your pocket for luck. Charge water with citrine and use that water to make peppermint tea for a money tea ritual. (This crystal is safe to place in water, but avoid extreme temperatures.)

Moon Phase:
Waxing moon

Rose Quartz
Promotes love, heals strained relationships, increases self love, and heals emotional wounds.

Uses:

Position rose quartz crystals on your crystal grid around a love-themed focal point. Carnelian pairs well with this stone when you're calling in a lover. Use this in a ritual bath with flower petals of your choice, pink Himalayan sea salt, sprigs of rosemary for the ultimate self-love spell. Make a rose quartz elixir by soaking the stone in a drink of your choice for at least twenty minutes. Drink the beverage when you are feeling sad, emotional, or feeling PMS symptoms. (This crystal is safe to place in water, but avoid extreme temperatures.)

Moon Phase:
New moon and waning moon

Turquoise

Healing, releasing unwanted energy, protects you from unwanted negative energy when you are meditating on your blocks or limiting beliefs.

Uses:
Hold this stone when you meditate and journal about limiting beliefs. Use in a crystal grid with amethyst and clear quartz with the intention to break bad habits, release unwanted thought patterns, or open your mind to more positive thoughts. Don't place this stone in water.

Moon Phase:
Waning moon

OILS BY MOON PHASE

(Check with a doctor before using any essential oil. This stuff is potent.)

New Moon
Sandalwood
Lemon
Melissa
Carrot Seed

∼

Waxing Moon
Pine
Wintergreen
Eucalyptus
Spruce

∼

Full Moon

Vanilla
Ginger
Frankincense
Cassia

∽

Waning Moon
Angelica
Cypress
Myrrh
Rose

∽

Any Moon Phase
Jasmine
Violet

∽

HERBS, RESINS + INCENSE BY MOON PHASE

(Use proper fire safety and ventilation when using herbs, resins, and incense. Don't light these around any children or pets.)

New Moon
Peppermint
Catnip Leaf
Chamomile
Lemon Verbena

Waxing Moon
Rosemary
Ginger
Echinacea
Rooibos

Full Moon
Horehound
Elderflowers
Chai
Rose Hip

∽

Waning Moon
Lavender
Passionflower
Chamomile
Sage
For Any Moon Phase
Jasmine
Dandelion

∽

FRUITS, VEGETABLES + SEASONINGS BY MOON PHASE

New Moon Energy

Fruit
Apples
Pears
Lemons
Melons

Vegetables
Celery
Tomato
Beans

Seasonings
Thyme
Clove
Cumin

∽

Waxing Moon Energy

Fruit
Pineapple
Strawberries
Blueberries
Blackberries

Vegetables
Onion
Peas
Broccoli
Cabbage

Seasonings
Cinnamon
Allspice

∽

Full Moon Energy

Fruit
Grapes
Bananas
Kiwi
Peach

Vegetables
Lettuce
Carrots
Potatoes
Squash
Pumpkin

Seasonings
Vanilla

∼

Waning Moon Energy
Fruits
Oranges
Mango
Lime
Plum
Raspberries
Cranberries

Vegetables
Garlic
Leek
Cauliflower
Mushrooms
Corn

Seasonings
Dill
Tarragon

∼

CHARGING MAGICAL TOOLS, WATER + EVERYDAY OBJECTS WITH MOON ENERGY

Because each magical tool holds a unique energy, there are certain moon phases that work better than others to charge each tool. Use this list to get some ideas for how to make the most of the moon's energy.

Note: The way I charge an object with moon magic is to leave it by a window or outside overnight. If I don't have that much time, I'll settle for leaving the object in the moonlight for twenty minutes.

Use this list to get some ideas for how to make the most of the moon's energy

- Charge pentagrams with **new moon** energy
- Charge athames with **waxing moon** energy
- Charge wands with **waxing moon** energy
- Charge tarot and oracle cards with **full moon** energy
- Charge candles with **full moon** energy
- Charge cauldrons with **full moon** energy

- Charge brooms with **waning moon** energy

Charging Water with the Moon to Make Moon Water

Water will take on the energy of any moon phase, making it an elixir that can be suitable for anointing magical tools, candles, drinking, diffusing, or charging/cleansing a sacred space.

Charging Everyday Objects with Moon Power

- Charge cell phones with **new moon** energy to cleanse it of any negative or unwanted energy it picked up throughout the month.
- Charge your car keys in **new moon** energy to protect you and set you on your journey with good intentions.
- Charge your wallet and/or money in **waxing moon** energy to call in more wealth and abundance.
- Charge wedding or party invitations in **full moon** energy so your guests can feel the celebratory energy as soon as they open the envelope.
- Charge your wedding ring or a trinket from your beloved in **full moon** energy to increase love and passion between you and your lover.
- Charge clothing in **waning moon** energy to release any negative energy that got stuck on it at some point in the month. Use this if you got in a fight or had a negative experience while wearing a certain article of clothing.
- Charge your journal in whatever energy you feel will best serve your latest journal entry. If you are

journaling about a list of goals or intentions, use **new moon** energy. If you're writing about getting a new job, increasing energy, or an investment, use **waxing moon** energy. If you're writing about something you want people to acknowledge and celebrate, charge it with **full moon** energy. If you're writing about problems, relationships issues, blocks, or any emotions you are trying to release, charge your journal in **waning moon** energy.

CONCLUSION

How are you feeling right now? Inspired? Overwhelmed? Intrigued by the possibilities of your personal moon practice?

My advice is start small by performing quick lunar spells that fit into your daily life like taking a moon bath or sipping moon water. Then, if you have the time and energy, try your hand at the more elaborate spells, like creating an altar for the current lunar cycle or writing your own moon spell.

Don't force yourself to perform lunar magic on days you don't feel like it. Remember how I was "white-knuckling" myself into alignment when I was working my crappy job?

Don't do that.

Be like the moon.

The moon knows it's OK to "go dark" sometimes because it will always once again shine bright!

Be gentle with yourself and listen to the rhythm of your own energy. You are always moving through different phases, just like the moon. Don't try to make yourself shine like a full moon every single night. It's unnatural, and it's a recipe for burnout.

You'll have days when you're full of energy and joy, but you'll also have days when you feel depressed, lazy, and barely able to muster up the energy to brush your teeth before crawling into bed.

For all your "dark" days, here's my list of very powerful, yet low-effort moon spells:

- Glance out the window and see if you can spot the moon.
- Google what the current moon phase of the moon is while you're lying in bed and think back over your day to see how the moon's energy has affected you.
- Drink water! The moon has a strong connection to water, so whenever you drink water, you are strengthening your personal connection to the moon.
- Look up your daily horoscope on your favorite astrology app.
- Whisper a secret to the moon.
- Thank the moon for quietly watching over you while you sleep—like a celestial Edward Cullen.
- Make "lazy" moon water. Place an empty cup, mug or water bottle on your windowsill to absorb the moon's energy. Even without the water, that moon's energy will charge the cup. Then when you pour your coffee the next morning, you can enjoy the benefits of moon water without all the prep!

How To Set Your Moon Practice Up For Success

A great way to stay consistent with your magic is to

create magical "kits" for yourself at the beginning of the month or lunar cycle.

For example, if you plan to do a weekly money ritual under the moon, fill a paper bag with all the items you need to cast that spell four times during that particular lunar cycle. You could fill that bag with four green candles (one for each time you perform the spell), a piece of citrine, and four of your favorite money-themed cards from your tarot deck (such as the Queen of Pentacles, The Magician, the Empress, and the Ten of Cups).

If you want to do a weekly ritual bath each lunar cycle, fill up four mason jars with all the ingredients you'll need for your soak, such as sea salt and dried lavender. Then you can simply pour your mixture into the bath and bask in the magic.

You can also buy full magical kits online or from a metaphysical store. They're a bit more pricey, but they can be convenient. I bought a bottle of self-love bath salt with dried herbs mixed in. It took all the guesswork out of my ritual baths on those nights when I was too tired to put something together myself.

Another option for the modern witch is to perform spells that don't require any tools! The moon bath meditation would fall into this category, as well as any meditating on any moon-themed affirmations. Put a reminder on your phone so you never miss out on adding a dose of magic to your busy life!

The last thing I want to ask you is, "What one bit of magic stuck with you the most after reading this book?"

I believe that the magical concepts and ideas that wedge themselves into your mind are the ones you should explore further. Usually, the magic that you need the most is the magic that you can't seem to get out of your head.

So what are you waiting for? Put down this book and go

cast that moon spell! It's time to co-create with the beautiful, abundant moon!

A Note From Julie Wilder

Thanks for picking up this book! I hope it helped you on your magical journey.

If you want to learn more ways to practice simple, secular witchcraft, be sure to pick up **a free copy of my book of spells, and my free Beginner Witch Starter kit with printables, correspondences, meditations, and magical journaling prompts.** Use the link below to get both of those!

https://whitewitchacademy.com/freebies

Also, be sure to check out the other witchy books in the **White Witch Academy Textbook series.** You can find them here:

https://whitewitchacademy.com/books

If you're on social media,
follow me on Instagram or Tik Tok **@whitewitchacademy**
Or send me an email at contact@whitewitchacademy.com

Lastly, **if you enjoyed this book leave a review so other witches can decide if this book is for them!** Reviews help me out so much and I appreciate the feedback.

Thank you for reading. I hope this book bought a little joy and magic to your life!

Until next time,

Julie Wilder xx

ALSO BY JULIE WILDER

What Type of Witch Are You?
How to Become A Witch
Why Didn't My Spell Work?
Beginner Witch's Guide to Grimoires
Tarot for Beginner Witches
Simple Moon Magic

Printed in Great Britain
by Amazon